Ducks

by Derek Zobel

BELLWETHER MEDIA · MINNEAPOLIS, MN

Note to Librarians, Teachers, and Parents:

Blastoff! Readers are carefully developed by literacy experts and combine standards-based content with developmentally appropriate text.

Level 1 provides the most support through repetition of high-frequency words, light text, predictable sentence patterns, and strong visual support.

Level 2 offers early readers a bit more challenge through varied simple sentences, increased text load, and less repetition of high-frequency words.

Level 3 advances early-fluent readers toward fluency through increased text and concept load, less reliance on visuals, longer sentences, and more literary language.

Level 4 builds reading stamina by providing more text per page, increased use of punctuation, greater variation in sentence patterns, and increasingly challenging vocabulary.

Level 5 encourages children to move from "learning to read" to "reading to learn" by providing even more text, varied writing styles, and less familiar topics.

Whichever book is right for your reader, Blastoff! Readers are the perfect books to build confidence and encourage a love of reading that will last a lifetime!

This edition first published in 2012 by Bellwether Media, Inc.

No part of this publication may be reproduced in whole or in part without written permission of the publisher. For information regarding permission, write to Bellwether Media, Inc., Attention: Permissions Department, 5357 Penn Avenue South, Minneapolis, MN 55419.

Library of Congress Cataloging-in-Publication Data
Zobel, Derek, 1983-
Ducks / by Derek Zobel.
   p. cm. – (Blastoff! Readers : Backyard wildlife)
Includes bibliographical references and index.
Summary: "Developed by literacy experts for students in kindergarten through grade three, this book introduces ducks to young readers through leveled text and related photos"–Provided by publisher.
ISBN 978-1-60014-596-4 (hardcover : alk. paper)
1. Ducks–Juvenile literature. I. Title.
QL696.A52Z63 2012
598.4'1–dc22   2011002251

Printed in the United States of America, North Mankato, MN.

080111   1187

Contents

Ducks are birds with **bills**. They **nest** on land and swim in water.

bill

Male ducks are called drakes. Females are called hens.

drake

hen

Ducks talk to
each other.
Hens quack.
Drakes use
other sounds.

9

Ducks nest in grasslands and **wetlands**. They live near lakes and rivers.

Ducks have **webbed feet**. They **waddle** when they walk.

**webbed
feet**

Webbed feet help ducks paddle in water. They also help ducks dive for food.

Ducks use their bills to grab food. They eat plants, worms, frogs, and small fish.

Ducks also
use their bills
to **preen**
their feathers.

Ducks make **oil** to put on their feathers. The oil makes their feathers **waterproof**. All dry!

Glossary

bills—the mouths of ducks

nest—to make a home

oil—a liquid that pushes away water; duck skin creates oil that makes duck feathers waterproof.

preen—to clean; ducks use their bills to preen their feathers.

waddle—to move with a side-to-side motion

waterproof—not able to get wet

webbed feet—feet with thin skin connecting the toes

wetlands—wet, spongy land; bogs, marshes, and swamps are all wetlands.

To Learn More

AT THE LIBRARY

Dunn, Judy. *The Little Duck*. New York, N.Y.:
Random House, 2008.

Pfeffer, Wendy. *Mallard Duck at Meadow
View Pond*. Norwalk, Conn.: Soundprints,
2001.

Sexton, Colleen. *Ducklings*. Minneapolis,
Minn.: Bellwether Media, 2008.

ON THE WEB

Learning more about
ducks is as easy as 1, 2, 3.

1. Go to www.factsurfer.com.

2. Enter "ducks" into the search box.

3. Click the "Surf" button and you will see a
   list of related Web sites.

With factsurfer.com, finding more information
is just a click away.

Index

The images in this book are reproduced through the courtesy of: Vasyl Helevachuk, front cover; Kosarev Alexander, p. 5; Andy Gehrig, p. 7; Minden Pictures/Masterfile, p. 9; Konrad Wothe/Minden Pictures, p. 11; Juan Martinez, p. 11 (left); Gerald A. DeBoer, p. 11 (middle); Galyna Andrushko, p. 11 (right); Thierry Van Baelinghem/Photolibrary, p. 13; Thomas Aichinger/Outdoor-Archiv/Alamy, p. 15; Sophie Bengtsson, p. 17; Josiah J. Garber, p. 17 (left); Matthijs Wetterauw, p. 17 (middle); Ilya D. Gridnev, p. 17 (right); S. Cooper Digital, p. 19; Luis Casiano/Photolibrary, p. 21.